Through a Window

Through a Window

Norman Fischer

ROOF BOOKS
New York

ISBN: 979-8-9896652-4-2
Library of Congress Control Number: 2024940156

Book design by Deborah Thomas

Acknowledgments
Parts of this poem appeared in the online magazines *Chant de la Sirene* and *Pamanar*. Thanks to editors Laura Hinton and Ghazal Mosadeq respectively. Thanks also to Ted Pearson and Hank Lazer who read the manuscript and provided astute and valuable tweaks.

NEW YORK STATE OF OPPORTUNITY. | Council on the Arts   This book is made possible, in part, by the New York State Council on the Arts with the support of Governor Kathy Hocul and the New York State Legislature.

Roof Books
are published by Segue Foundation
300 Bowery Fl 2
New York, NY 10012
seguefoundation.com

For book orders, please go to Roofbooks.com

You are so alone in this lovely world

>Friederich Holderlin
>(trans. Chernoff and Hoover)

acacias yellow now

lightpainted

things to see that are there

                              beyond

eye through window — distancegrey

        rock's there

              tree trunk's   there

patch of sky, blue

                    there, there

        T H E R E

& her laughing scorning voice

what others may think to do there

        a deer's there

placid grazing digesting there

    there under low branch soft earth shelter

where they rest safe at night

(3/21/20)

———

slightly branchtip wavings

    pittosporum, eucalyptus

      living's mantled waverings

fenced with wood railing

    pip pip pip's heat

life's, fluid

    Cloud. Cover. But

small blue sky patches

    distanceseen beyond the

        eye

    sees as distance as nor flat

      but space as

mind's hand's writing space

    sound of it lifted over ground

    green, white, blue

lit by celestial above

        as dry leaf floats

      across view

        narrow brown

   passionate gone

(3/22/20)

———

Sun!

  this further painting

maybe things click, hum

in mind, whir

      as backstage

    machinery

brass doorknob guards

human thought, passion

from punishing elements

hope, hype — 's likewise

that : eyes draw shape

paint color from bounced dark light

from meaning's

feeling's

memory frames

personal symphonic score

then plays piece

(3/22/20)

——

So different looking close
at something within reach
an object to be domesti-
cated one can grip
history in persons/
places/tales/memory in looking
through distancespace at what's
not gripped in hand
from where it cannot
thus by hand be sub-

sumed has nor shimmering
presencehistory in space
no past looking
brings to mind another music
held in breathless heartbeat with
all my soul with
all my might

(3/22/20)

——

some somber but bright

light

    's brighter in written or less...

        beeping truck's

all over movement one sees

one says one sees (in mind

    says writes

    in further moment)

s e e s

s e e s

    eye's everywhere moving

in pittosporum's wavering

squirrel on wooden railing

no sooner there than going

written

(3/23/20)

———

Wind!

(whistles, whips)

W. I. N. D.

early in   waking dawn

roof's rainsound

whitewater flows on wood railing

almost seen

again seen

in looking in hearing

thumps heartbeat

making *rain* in mind

imagining wet to go outside

is wet there   beyond

window's soak swelling

wind window wet wild

in mind's sounding

damp inside body

the more insistent thought of it

drops flying off taller in

deeper depressions

yet light

blaze

in chill day

in sharp points nearly seen

width of wood railing

sheltering dry boards

beneath

almost

(3/24/20)
——

suddenly sun painting

yellow light moment

opens ecstatic mental tubes

to modulate fog-filled sun-

light diffuse mellow

blaze in middle distance

not dancing on railing

sparrows peep out

sparkle on leaftips

like conductor's hand waving

across orchestra, fog whisps

sweeps close in

distance sparkles

too on pittosporum's

looking makes full

in words' minds

(3/24/20)

———

ethereal light on

shining leaves

under rain

glinting in variegated spots

on curved pale green long

eucalyptus leaves

white branches strain stretch in wind…

grey gradually

returns in light

dims day to earthbound

moments flash

(3/24/20)

———

looking underlies unity in

    heart, sky

looking's innate impulse

    toward wholeness

dusty window

    waters splotches, cob-

       webs

    blind 1/3 drawn

       leaves many vague

       black

    shaded reflections

(Mei-mei's *Treatise on Stars*)

(3/25/20)

———

some greens yellows

    some greys or grays

some blacks where leaf's

edge rhymes with

tree's bark or space between

[is   space   Black

Is It   White.   Grey?

gray   is   white

with black   or

Black with White??

Sun/day   or   its   absence/night

but there's   no   night,   no   day

One. Sees. In   some.   Times   ]

railing like eyes

horizontal

trees like nose

vertical

(3/25/20)

—–

Crow caw

   Engine whine

  Pen scratch

           paper

or so people say not scratch

but abstract sound registers symbol

     some meanings

       ear

makes a living ear

that time occurs in it[*if*

   no event   then

       no   time]but this

seeing : seeing blank

space seeing white

page become sensible

speaking[*refrigerator*

sound] barely some leaves

move

mid-pittosporum

(3/25/20)

——

Whisper cloud above hori

    zontal in pale

       blue barely

  white or   barely

         gray

 whipping eu

    calyptus tops

in winds whispers

   dashing across shak

    ing

toss

           ing big loose tops

in delicate

white topmost

    branchlets

        speaking ...

(4/1/20)

———

in midst of dense
[any word amazes]
eucalyptus foliage
fulfills visual

    seeing only graygreen

        moving

in shattering wind crossing

           some yellow at top with

some sun beginning

    to move above distant

        hill

and some light come

      In.   ***In.***

   open   spaces

in foliage day's

beyond it all

to

come

(4/1/20)

———

Memorializing sun blaze

On ocean can't see

Eye registers an edge

Or it's pain to look

Mauve hills backdrop

Foreground background

Unground

Recollection in tranquility

In writing mind's

Eyes

(4/3/20)

———

Silver metallic blaze

    At angle on desk

    Close in looking

Paper arrangements

        Staples frog

In own shadow

In light all's

        Dark

Blinded by light

Light speaks

    Says light, light

There's always no shape

      Ever

(4/7/20)

———

Some white some

    blue some black

some some some

ever some never

some blue or white all —

some music in some

seeing

some space there or here

between branches

some   space

knows   space

knows one, someone

clusters of leaves

Hang down

In?   *In?*

(4/7/20)

——

Minute changes

[no such]

these shadows

eternally darken

grow long fingers

[no such]

black greenly

movement darker

over   metal   beasty

factual   factual

world

(4/10/20)

———

Half pulled back

jagged shocked red

smearing swirls

shivering, scratching

junco tail twitching sheathed white

hopping ever quizzical

flits on pittosporum branch

gone.......

then branchtip aftertwitter

in brisk blustering

windy

higher, eucalyptus branches

swish insistent

behind

either all sky

as beyond

or sky pieces

as between

there's not there

and is

and moves and

(4/10/20)

———

Monochrome

   grey light   not

    dark in day

handwritten script

  flourish in hand

leaves barely stir

  but stir barely

something stirs barely

   some small small strip

        somewhat seems to stir simple

nor flag nor wind nor

mind:

     hand

(4/17/20)

———

Shrouded im

  mobile auto

mobile

sleek, dark, horizontal

swells upward

as snake

swallows elephant

in her sublunar

face one sees

green curved

branch

white

skywatch

scatter

reflects

(4/17/20)

———

Trees' trunks strain

toward descriptive words

sloped hillside

stuttering attention

knobby grasses twitch

just slight

slight/slant/stark

straight they're

straight

forward

neither guile nor gull

nor

dissemble nor stammer

flat strap leaves

flop over rock

R o c k t

S t a r k

R o c k

lavender bunch

(4/21/20)

———

Tall black pine

      pale blue sky beyond

   fore or back

    ground

     incant mind

    moves slight slant

     in wind seen

      nor felt

    each side

     of

    wind

     ow

(4/21/20)

———

Garden gate

beyond porch

   rail

  light beyond

   dark wood

plum tree full

    green in o

pen

    light

beyond, tall

     dark

     pine

rail

gate

plum

pine

dark

        in light

     iris

(4/21/20)

——

Unseen fly buzz

   crossing wood beams

unlike sunbeams

   now   visible   fly
      now not

Looking *up* looking

     down

Fly's purpose

   wor   ds

  dis   inte

    grate

    grate

 on tongue

nothing so obvious

in the way of

(4/22/20)

———

Golden doorknob

    in

  side

    out

  side

    your

  side

    my

  side

Slightly stirring plum branch

  lit yellow green

  there's no certain

    color but eye

    we say's

  the standard name

    porch railing

    wood:

gate, o

pen

one, not six twists

(4/22/20)

——

Low   lavender   clump

where's human interest/tale

in slightly moving wind

   dumb plants

no wanting

  where's plot

    of land

    curve of old

    acacia trunk

     twists

  reach

      out   up

in   to

Still nondrama

(4/22/20)

———

Pine tree   bark

dark on south

west side

in some splotch

pale blue sky patch

beyond

space

all in brain

all in mind's

eyes' pool

Abstract?

drawn away

by eye

Abstract perception

Abstract expression

    ab stract

    ob struct

    in   struct

    ob ject[*hurl*]

         enfolded structures///

(4/22/20)

———

Shadow painted dark

    on slope where yellow

      grass patch

    made dark there

assumption

    in perception

    sneaky tricks, sleight of hand in eye ear words

Such honest stone!

Not fooling

anyone

Blades of grass

B l a d e s ? ?

G r a s s ? ?

(4/22/20)

———

Dark pine , pittosporum

in pale sky foreground

background cloud streaks

beyond

distancethink

eucalyptus branch

twitchsway in wind

[*breeze* better]

some [other branch] Eu-

Cal

Ip

Tus

Long curved leaves as swords

Blackgreen , in Clust

Ers

wave maybe

Good-bye?

(5/5/20)

———

Updown   or

backforth eucalyptus

leaves wave long slender

clusters

at   end   of

thin branchlets

limply receptive

to airwaft no

resistance

Who's   here

in   them   these

words' leaves

dumb but

Yawping

(5/5/20)

———

Evening: deep blue

dark blue sky

in patches between

black trees

staid or weary

Room's reflection

in window

electric light

     makes somber color

  The

   writing

   self's

  its mastermatter

slave to inner space

  takes dictation

outside recedes from

        thought

(5/14/20)

———

Bright   air   yellow   lit

   cloud   white

 not a whit of fur

or machinery whir

as silence swallows time's

thought

Eu

Cal

Yp

Tus,

pittosporum

leaves

delicate

wagglesway

in hushing

wind's

hovered breath

(5/19/20)

———

Sleek low auto

mobiles lurk

cantilevered

on concrete parking platform

such words written by

        H   A   N   D

don't resolve to

        page photo

graphs

all round in green

  leaves, trees's leaves

in bunches on branches

    and bluesky patch

beyond

squirrel lopes by

(5/19/20)

———

spotted fawn — now

    two faun(s)(*headsmouthslegs*)

jerklook up one then

graze now black nose in grass

other then

mother long legged

ahead, neck

stretched long tail

twitch

walks slow beyond jerklooks

up to

side jerk, silent *what, what?* eye

new motion

less in sun

gently frames female body

(5/20/20)

——

same lightpatch

Same. Old. Trees?

or some

                    trees

                                    or

            acacia, pine, pittos

                porum   furzed

        gray   swatch

                as gorse

        gray light stanchion

                helmeted

        (there before but not seen till now)

        perfect light lit

        felt tip view

        (6/4/20)

        ———

                        no

                movement

                Just.   Now.

        Now.   Something.   Moves.

movement   moves

some. Branchlet

shift shift

continuous

here here

in pittosporum

slow still quiet twitch

no person animal poet

colors somber

(gray   green   brown

black) save for

red traffic cones

seen tween brown

fence slats

(6/8/20)

———

fence slats thick in fore

      ground. Left. To. Right.

behind thick fence slats horizontal below

      diagonal   con

          verging

 rhymed shadows

        sun paints at distance precise

geometric demarcate garden green,

    full, some

white tipt feverfew

green. tarpaper. roof.

beneath fully leaved

plum tree

slightly curved

eucalyptus bole

>W H I T E<

beyond day's last

seen sun

(6/8/20)

———

Earlier, memory

Of strong sunlight on

Yellow grasses whipt

In this and that way

In sea's wind

O such grasstips

Thought, O lovely

Lovely little blades!

So earnestly doing

Being whipping

Whipped in air

Twisting trees there

Hill's curve

Eye, memory

Writing memory

and writing

&

(6/8/20)

———

Big rocky hills' rough brow

At distancehaze of

Some lingering last light

Lonely bench there

No one from it looking

At space below

Where waves' crush (memory though

Can't now see) batters rock

Long long before people

Some brightness ahead

Horizon obscured by boles,

leaves, boles

(6/8/20)

———

NEARLY NOW DARK SKY WHITE
PEARL GRAY OR PALE PALE
BLUE BEHIND BLACK BLACK TREE
REFLECTION SELF IN WINDOW
THICK DARK TREES TO LEFT
PATCHES OF SAME LIGHT
FADING SHOW THROUGH GAPS
ALL'S BROODING OVER EYE OF
EARTH LOOKING SPIKEY CYPRESS
BRANCHES SLIGHTLY TWITCH
SILENCE IN SPECTATORSHIP
DAY'S FALLING LOW NOW
IN ORIGINAL TIME'S GAP

(6/9/20)

———

Star K White

Opium poppies

>_Tall_<

>_Spindly_<

Sway. In. Foggy. Wind. whipt

as flag snaps

for united poppy state

her universal citizen,

a

cloud,
staggers

above

brown grasses sadly

endure

gray sky

fuzzed in fog

(7/17/20)

———

Poor cypress large limb

Cut[*raw*]

Scattered rocks

One by one approach wind

Ow

Not moving

or indicating

Names

Names of things
Names of actions
Names of conditions, states

Dead grasses small/straight

Twitch

Hold fast

Gray succulent beyond/tall

Sky beyond

(7/17/20)

———

White. Sky. Up. Over

      there

  through

           weather-eaten

                      wind

                                  ow

have stomach, finger

         eye to see

    all over slightly twitching

[in wind, small]

         pittosporum neat

        green leaves

  bunchy like hair

    on head's unruly

(7/20/20)

——

Narrow.　Hori

　　　　Zon

　　　　　　Tal

　　　　　　　　　Win

　　　　　　　　　　　　Dow

[wind

　　ow ?]

full of leaves, boles

Pittosporum , pine

　　　　　Eu

　　　　　　　Cal

　　　　　　　　　yptus

Small white sky beyond holds
Only one small hanging
Eucalyptus

Leafbatch
Very slight wag

(7/20/20)

———

Smeared window
Fog or light rain
[the singers....]
Reaching out cypress branch
In fog or light rain
Seen through...

Suppressed speech
Surpassed speech
Can't say what think
Round tones —

Criss-crossed branches
Thick branch thin
Branch could snap

In winter wind

Rock

Grass

(7/21/20)

———

Fence rail close in field
Wide, horizontal, brown, worn
With horizontal wooden cap, vertical
Member bolted, four
Bolts, further back in field gray wood
Fence top to which
Wire's affixed, big wooden
Gate, plum tree bare now
Of white flowers, red plums

Cypress trees green behind—
White sky surrounds beyond

(7/26/20)

——

Thick tree's stump
Brown hills fall
At angles
Slope up, down

All branches of
Acacia, cypress
Move in mind
Steady, slight

Rhyming [boles]
Small, large
Rocks gray, white
Only there, here

In significant
Pattern Wagner's
Music's fury
Mimics

(7/26/20)

——

Weather's slow dance
Grabs a word
In situ

Strapped to
Obscured picture
Of what's beyond that door

Sky disclosed trees
In sight's slight
Naming brain

Hearty world calls
Enthusiastically
To circus performer

(7/26/20)

——

vus.   machsdu

vus.   viltzdu

here

mistook tree for word

living tree

slowly

drinks sea's salt wind

blows across plain

under fog-obscured sun

entire unseen

but breathing

unseen sea's wash

casts mood

(7/26/20)

———

Writing while walking
Backforth steps
One foot in front of
Other — then exchange
See window before
Then behind cuts off
Pittosporum's top

Framed white
Clean shape

But tree's outside
In air's space's complex
Shapes — stop. Look.

(7/27/20)

——

Fence slats/thick thin

Thick/horizontal

    Vertical

Light stanchion/

               helmeted—

    Gray metal slight

      ly

          tilts

behind this one green

    acacia burst not

moving/pittosporum

    leaves close in mov

      ing more than

slightly in

Wind : gray day [mar-

    rine   layer]

(7/27/20)

——

Morning. —   all afternoon

Early morning /. Late

    Morn

     Ing

Early.   After

           noon   then

Late afternoon then

    even

         ing/dusk

Then. Sun. Sets. It's

dusk dusk dusk

                    light thins slow drains flees

        dusky dusk

    dust or dusk dimming

— then night , early

night late night

dark night with or

    with — out

        stars, moon, clouds

        that thin

spread over

        take. Dark. Till

dawn's gonna

break—

The broken dawn

(7/27/20)

——

quiet graywhite

sky, some   sky

there over beyond

living things

beyond living things
mauve metal water's color

black / dark blue

greens of foliage —

just to name this and that

in English language little

plain words…

overall movement means

times pass

(7/29/20)

———

evening : some

   pale   purple

   sky late in the
       in the

in   the

day, late in the day

late in the day

   the waning

   of the

               light

  one pale orange

   sunpatch in crook

of eucalyptus limb

   dusky green dark green

lower or higher

trembling leaves

(7/29/20)

———

black   tree

barely   moves

pale   purple   sky

wide   open   sky   arms

welcome!

but

music's playing

voices singing

in   the

overarched silence

no birds

chirp

late in the day

late in the day

the quiet day

    fading

(7/29/20)

———

Recline from another angle
Over sky in time's delight
See new picture fresh view
Holy Holy Holy
Lucia de Lammermoor's gone mad
Suppose
I have name of that tree
Wrong it's another tree
Another name does it matter
Which impression one has
It is yours

Not flowering now.
Bark scored.
Invisible to reader
No matter the word
Picture in mind
Pigmy nuthatch slate
Grey and white and cute and squat
Jerky and perky
Just as real

(8/2/20)

———

Plum tree whacked by light!
Its greens now yellow as this year's thin
Canes sway in little breeze
Plums all gone red red shiny
And sweet they were baskets
Of them falling when shake tree
And boiled and froze and et
Some blue sky after fog days
Weeks of sacred marine layer
Ocean's revenge on land
Land's caress of sea
How white the peeled eucalyptus
Bark how grateful the day
O leaves and trunks your
Bundled enigmas draw one
To feet in kudos and applause
Late day's light-filled fullness

(8/2/20)

———

Whine of leaf blower's meaning
Altered now blows away toxic
Gas police deploy in Portland
Two kinds pittosporum nearly
Meet in path's midst
Some white skypatch between
They stretch forward each
As poor lovers' forbidden reach
In tragic opera they love as
Desperately just cause they
Can't set up house have coffee
Toast send kids to school they
Die/Die as music crashes down
At end curtain falls we
Audience sadly reflect how
Pale our life at least though
We live, acacia's paler green beyond
Them beyond that more sky

(8/10/20)

———

wide grey-white sky fills view

red bush, spiked leaves

rose in late bloom round

    edges

   of   sky

   goes   on

flat there

fog blows across

smudgy eucalyptus in

dist

ance

wind   blows

in bitter damp

twitches patient leaves

(8/11/20)

——

Lightning!   Wind!   Rain

pelts down sudden

sudden stopping

pelting stopping

Then Sun! Bright!!

gathering thunder loud

in near, far, distance

some drop then tap then drum

    on roof

fence slats light, shaded

    light changes, bright/

      somber looms

   strong quiet then

    silent then loud

for afternoon

(8/16/20)

——

Pink. Naked. Ladies

Blown. Slightly

In somber light

Beneath lichen-stained

Acacia trunk

Before big pine stump

Curve of hill

Falling, Unmoving

Toward hale coast

Live oak's

Low hung

Branch

Dark

Green

Monterey cypress looms

Above before white

Sky expecting nothing

Receiving just that

Much in frozen

Time's (*summer*)

(8/16/20)

———

sudden splash of bright

light on all eucalyptus

boles   sharp   white

illumined

noble, tall, still

against yellow *(now*

as written

changed — white)

sky

beyond

[sky holds as if in

open-armed contain
                        ment]

widespread scope

of Monterey cypress

darkest green

before, below

it

(8/16/20)

—-

Little. Sun. Orb. Up

In sky.   Over hill

Smudged in fog smoke

Somber light makes

Evening noon

Noon evening

Sky's not following sky

Rules!

Dark in the day time

Slow   slow   turns

Earth   aside

now(later)

Quiet white end of

Day   sky

Earth enters peace

in all.

(9/11/20)

——

Some birds peep

Soot's coat's everywhere

But fussy quail with

   Circle hats brown black fat

Strut and muster

   Small family group

      noisy busy

     Trees solemn

       don't or do

       care

    in their tree manner

Shape's quiet music

   as green speak

or brown in bole

  or stripped bark

    white or yellow

peeled

as eye or

apple

(9/11/20)

———

suntinted leaves

green or black

twitch in pittosporum

red's fence rail slats/fence slats rail

and open spaces showing

what's beyond —

objects in occupying space

stop it?

take it up?

squeeze it?

But without them

space's blank

appearance devoid

till object behind beyond

    and in and as

   stops — another

spacious day slides by

(9/15/20)

——

Fall — a new wind

    ow

In/on time's pass

   age

Narrow horizontal
Fence rails
See lower part of gate
See light there in
World there see words
Here describing
And not garden plants
Not moving in misty gray
Foggy day green they are
And gray or shade half
Pulled down after a time

To return not yet ready
For what's to be see in death

(10/18/20)

———

Evening's dark light
Covers sleek fox body
Moving left to right past window
Makes sudden passing
Obscure/cypress branches'
Emotion against indigo
Sky desk lamp light pool
Makes outdoors dreamy dark
A quiet ethereal
More and less real than thought
Nothing moves when time's stopped
If no wind now
Where owls hoot
Is yellow or slight
Drop of white in dark sky
Gleams
Where last of settled sun or
First of risen moon
(Quarter full) begins its
Influence/each instance what
Light's here lessens what
Dark becomes dream
Approach in mind's swerve
Toward night's coming

(10/11/20)

———

Live light mist creeps

Across image birds

Chirp silver or car's

Silver cover blurs

Edges like obscure car

ghost tree's limbs barely

move — now light's

brighter a moment

then again not

in general silence

what's stopped mind

look listen

to wheeling world's

motion/time

falling slowmo off

cliff where we live

(10/20/20)

———

leaves. on. leaves

in layers of leaves

some   brown

pine needle clumps

one. thin. acacia. branchlet

with delicate leaves lacy

against grayblue sky

O you are such an

excitement little

nuthatch fussing

and poking here and there

(10/20/20)

——

shouting world's

elsewhere — dusky mauve

sky surrounds

somber leafy trees

lamp's reflection

    (circle of light above)

in reflection so one

      sees

inside/outside

   in   one

     glass

  quiet evening

last birdsong

(11/4/20)

———

no. people. in. this

picture:

good.   No.   One

needs them now as

evening draws down early

gathering mild darkness in

around tree's shoulders

like a cloak

Tree limbs eloquent

make emotional

appeal   to

supposed poet for

one must be

writing reading this

(11/4/20)

——

Big. High. Wind

    wagging cypress

        branches

pale   blue

    S.   K.   Y.

    beyond...

words   not   pictures

pictures   not   words

    blowing away all

        human scent stink

    in freshfresh

        air

Brown hillside falls to

    sea

not moving

(11/6/20)

———

dumb   pine stump

    solid..........still.......

below slightly moving

litgreen   acacia

    branches

above. Falling brown

hillside stubbled grasses

and

      twitching

   cypress branches

across in foreground

only a little

in wind/light

  Shadow across

(11/6/20)

———

sublime line

horizon's white blue

nonline mind

made

as wind whips big

whipping limbs

patient trees

need not practice

to know how to bend

stir

they stir bend

in wind's kiss

a

bracing

embracing

analogy in knowledge

(11/16/20)

———

past bloom'd succulent's

    thin stalks

   twitch slightly

in today's — now's —

   wind   called

  wind but there's

       no

       such

       just

    things move

     in rhythm

      such

      evidence

      such

         bustle

(11/16/20)

  ——

fall's thick shadows

paint on sloping hill

day's new : no

leaves on plum

tree thin

canes wave at

sky coming down

to meet

all-over-trees'

movement

top-swaying

roots I know push in deep

dark earth

hold them

here/ how

(11/16/20)

———

green roof below

fence lines intersect

this looking /seeing

this mixing words in

a

brain or mind or —

of whose coincidence

thin venting pipes

vigorous

sway in wind

(air's rapid moving

going all across

not arriving

sun's light lights

It up [*up?*]

here beyond

text

(11/16/20)

——

same still wind

ow

but move

chair's a different

view

one word after

the

other

pittosporum's top cropped

by window's upper

edge

acacia's yellow leaves

stir in sun then

stop stirring

pen 'n paper flow

endearing

(12/4/20)

———

narrow band of "view
from horizontal window" with
shades half drawn so "only
narrow band of" view
jumble of fence/ gate
straps of green "leaves
some white sky peeps" through
slate outside inside day
leaks last night's absent
light onto now all's
quiet but for pen's "scratch
on soft paper people" pass
in other places pass "on we
say pass" away
narrow band of view "life's
thinking feeling" pre
paring for next day "life
some white sky peeps" through
slats outside inside day

(12/4/20)

———

"O that fog bank above
sky's deep clear blue"
"starkly trees sharply
etched against it"
"white-barked eucalyptus
branched and gently curved
out toward   space"
"O the trees the trees
the trees the trees"

"and below green pines
bunched and cypress
jutting outward"
"sky's a hero, trees a
damsel on white
horse held by him
in silence" "whose
house is this whose
window?"

(12/10/20)

————

Catching flash in distance
Of early morning window
Blaze yellow there beyond
Myrtle tree on hillside
Tight foliage slightly moves
And bright orange spike
Of succulent massive
Stump of old pine and
Twisted limbs of acacia
In very pale light
Who's in charge here?
From whence did the visuals
Arrive to tap-tap the brain
Giving a feeling of world?

(12/26/20)

————

Beyond the yellow blaze of lamp
On desktop pale light
Other side of window
Blushed from sky where
Pine and cypress limbs
Slightly move in tiny breeze
That early light's tender-
Seeming lain down on
Soft ground
As light blanket
Over sleeping child
Much loved
Inside you feel and don't
Feel the brisk air but
Imagine and remember such
Grey-rough heavy
Cypress branches
Diagonal outside window
Are silent not moving
At
All

(12/26/20)

———

Mighty window's opaque
See only self's reflection
Person on chair pen in
Hand notebook on lap
Tonsu behind writing
Words in head or hand
Person's got head hand
Leg meaning shoes pants

Shirt image in glass
Color or no color there
But barely. Things so
Quiet just there night's
Just there so quiet what's
Quietly there, person, pen
Poem's reflection

(1/4/21)

—

Sun paints day outside
Inside sun paints day
Inside/outside painting
Day on both sides' wind
Ow — pittosporum barely
And widely, rarely, in
Breeze moves slow what's
Moving or movement in yell
Ow light chill in air
Winter's day — acacia
In middle distance (as
Seen from words' here)
Blazes brightly yellowing
Pale cloud filled sky be
Yond at far distance such
Are that which one is
Said to see so sees

(1/5/21)

——

Pale sky-patch between
Tree branch has nothing
To do with death of friend
Everything to do
Still sky's as ever
In flux constant coming
Going appearing disappearing
Seeming reliable and com
Forting has nothing to do with
Everything to do with
Human feeling about death
Of friend loved and known

Fifty or so years lived within
Metaphor or archetype or concept
As trees and pale sky
Coming and going through days and
Nights giving way to same and
New expressions, expressions

(For Mel 1/7/21)

———

(New window…)
Mauve or pearl sky
Full of cloud promising rain
(Or so forecasts say they change
All the time as the un
Expected occurs with
Regularity) soft folds of hills
Red leaves green leaves
Of tall and short plants
"Lucia! Lucia!"
Cascade of human feeling
Washed over rocks distorted
By them gathering to
Torrents these political
Times, hills, clouds,
Leaves

(1/28/21)

———

Corner of house sharp
Roof angle like sharp

Ankle bone of dangling
Foot distant eucalyptus
Tree's fussy pompous
Leaf crown from and to
Which twittering siskin
Flit in great sky's
Swoop as music
Swells stately and serious —
Winter bushes don't care
Green leaves there hang
From twisted twigs
Making garden shapes
As sudden light sweeps
Scene brightening it
While poor human swoons
Moodflitting in lightshift

(1/28/21)

———

Fence railing horizontal
Dark wood because sun's
Behind, above, not pouring
Light but backlit what
Could *backlit* mean when
Everything's in front or *en*
Face du le soleil here on
Earth
Earth
Cypress needles dark dark
Greenyellow in full sun
White bole of eucalyptus
Same in sunlight pale blue

Sky beyond shattering
Orange pyramidal aloe
Flowers bloom in full light
On hillside

(2/2/21)

———

Same window
Different angle/ankle
Can see ankle of crossed leg
If not looking out window where one
Sees over top of covered car
(In silver sheer plastic
Material blows off constant
In any wind) tree that's black
Not green because backlit
I mean tree's trunk tree's
Leaves pittosporum fence
Rail in sunlight front of
Car's cover blazes yellow white
In strong sun and yes yes
Again again
As ever (ever?)
Pale blue sky beyond

(2/10/21)

———

look into that piec e
of sky fragile opaqu e
heartbreak pale blu e

with bird or tw o
flits by in it — see tha t
wonder whether saw o r
not dark backlit smal l
birdlet though can hea r
many such sam e
in above tree s
stained red (that i s
stained red wood stained suc h

for preservatio n)
little porch don't se e
throug h
window but throug h
door opened throug h
which can se e
what's otherwise not see n
behind white close d
door but ye s
now porc h
shadow fencerail car s
criss-crossin g
tree s

(2/10/21)

―――

Blaze of light ball of
Above can't look at
Honey cream over all yellow
Is yellows it some dis
                              tance
Sound of scraping or loading
Unloading truck is it truck
This light makes all
                              in
Foreground dark because
Backlit light light renders
Objects fading as if shrink
                              ing
In fright of light greed envy
Idleness gluttony lustfulness
And more riding in on strange

Beasts the more light the
More shad

                          ow

(2/17/21)

——

The crouching lion there
Jammed up against dark
Shapes of visual a tree
Grows out its head
Some bird flies this and that
Way in very light blue sky
Holds it all in its beyond
As words suggest beyond for this
Story of temptation of knowledge
As eros desperate unless
Some simple story of those
One knows or knew forgotten
In immediacy of such writing
Such seeing such feeling of warm
On chest on sunny daylight
Focused by window on one
Squinting eye

(2/17/21)

——

Narrow horizontal band

                        of
Window with bar

                      in

                    center

Metal bar
                                        in

            center self
                                        in

            center as bar

making picture blind
Half drawn as eye half open
Horizontal lines of fence slats
Of retaining wall grid of wire
Mesh fencing tacked between
Four by fours red with wood stain
Before green plants some
Mess of plants behind and
Slats of formal gate thick
Posts to hold
                            it (the wall)

                    up

                    holding in turn

In turn dirt
Behind to make flat area
Where'd otherwise be slope

(2/17/21)

——

O falling hillside curves

steep in full light

behind—

wavering cypress

branches

twitch with vigor in

Brisk. Ocean. Air Some

gray , pale gray

succulents at wind

ow's

edge to far left

and yes the little green

grass blades also

twitch flexible

Nature: windowbedient

(2/20/21)

———

Now weathered face

    where heavy cypress trunk's

been

      lopped off but main

cypress trunk shaggy-barked

    muscles up to skycap

      hidden by win

            dow's

     top edge

smaller branches wave

    to right

flutter stretch out

        above grasses and

   strapleaved iris

without flowers this time

   of year — sun patch

   Beyond

(2/20/21)

——

Light's gathered to paint

Where

Plum tree's fresh

                    in

        Bloom [white

                petals on gray

        Wood mottled with greeny lichen

Old plum cut back strong

thought dead

and

                seemed

                        so

        two years

then burst forth bloom

        last   year

        and   copious

                plums

then

and back again   now

with sunlit bloom

Their

Day

> back. Again. Now<

(3/5/21)

ROOF BOOKS

the best in language since 1976

Recent & Selected Titles

More information on titles
can be found at Roofbooks.com

To order, please go to
Roofbooks.com